Who will listen to me?

JUDITH MATTISON

Art by Judy Swanson

AUGSBURG PUBLISHING HOUSE
MINNEAPOLIS, MINNESOTA

WHO WILL LISTEN TO ME?

Contents

To my mother
Junice Marie Magnuson Nelson
1915 - 1958
who listened to me
with love and understanding

Preface

We often think of prayer as an experience separated from daily life. We confine our prayers to church worship services or bedtime hours. But prayer is possible at any time. We believe that God is always present, so it is possible to pray—to think in the presence of God—at any moment.

We think and talk with God at private times, but also when we are with friends, when we are upset or worried, when we are driving or studying or thinking about our future. Conversations with God are unlimited in number or topic. Whatever is important to us is important to God, who loves us and wants to help us. As we struggle through life and experience many feelings and thoughts, God is present. Let's talk to God now.

JUDITH MATTISON

I'm glad to have my friend

I'm so glad to have a friend,
one close friend
who listens
and helps me figure things out.

I need someone
who doesn't leave when I act dumb
or when I'm grouchy,
who doesn't laugh at me.

I need someone who
is human around me
makes mistakes too
asks questions like mine
offers suggestions
can tell me true feelings.

I'm glad for a person to
do things with
talk with
complain to
be quiet with (for a change).

When I think of friends,
I think Jesus must have been the best,
the most loyal and loving.
Everybody needs a friend.

School seems like a prison

There is an order to everything.
Rules
"good reasons"
someone "in charge"
"through channels."

School gets to be like a prison
or a maze
where I can't do anything new
or different
or unusual.

I have to check everything
with someone else—
from lunchtime
to hall passes
to scheduling.
I feel so trapped!

I don't always agree
that the "solid, tested way"
is best.
I'm tired of inheriting rules.
I want to break out.

Jesus felt that way too.
And Martin Luther King
and Gandhi
and Lucy Stone.

They had good, genuine causes.
They changed things peacefully
by being persistent
loving
committed.

What am I trying to change
and what are my reasons?
Am I just rebellious
or are my causes worthwhile?
Help me keep my reasons and my methods worthy.

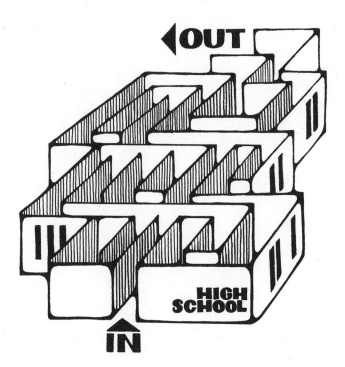

I'm scared of boys

I don't feel confident with boys.
I want to impress them
but when they're around
I can't think of things to say.
I'm especially uncomfortable with boys I like.

I always got along all right
when I used to play softball
or work on a science project with boys.
But now that kids are dating
I'm scared.

Usually I don't really want to date—
to go out alone with a boy.
I'm more comfortable in groups of kids.
But sometimes I do want to.
I guess I have to wait
until I feel less self-conscious.
I'll get used to boys.
Maybe they're just as scared of me!

My parents don't understand

My parents mean well.
They want to help me.
They want the best for me.
I'm sure they love me.
But my parents don't understand.
They see me through the eyes
of their teenage years.
Things are different now.
Kids today have new problems.

I try to tell my parents how I feel
but sometimes I can't.
I end up not talking
or else shouting
or being sarcastic.

Lord, I don't want to hurt them
but I have to be myself.
Help my parents realize
I can't always be like them.
I can't tell them
everything I do
or say
or think about.

Help me too, Lord.
Keep me from being unkind
when I talk with them.
And help me be a little more patient.

My parents mean well.
Maybe I can find ways
to help them understand.

I feel great!

Oh! Wow!
I got an invitation!
I feel great!
Life is exciting—
life is good.
I'm happy!
I want to shout at the night
and laugh with morning!
I want to hug someone.
Thank you
thank you
for life!

It's easy to gossip

Lord,
I feel ugly inside.
I just spent a whole evening
talking about other people.
I criticized
and complained
and even laughed behind the backs
of people who call me a friend.

I'm lacking something, Lord.
I don't feel whole.
Sometimes I feel more important
when I chip away at others.
I boost myself up
by deflating my friends.
I feel ashamed.

I know I have faults.
People could easily criticize me too.
I would feel hurt if I found out
others talk cruelly about me.

Lord, help me see ahead and realize
that my gossip does not build me up at all.
It hurts others
and makes me sour inside.

I want to be popular

Lord,
if I could wish for anything
I'd want to be popular.
I envy kids
who feel confident
who date a lot
who know how to make friends and wear clothes.
Sometimes my envy is near hate.
I despise their success.

Lord,
I wonder if I really hate myself
not them.
I'm disappointed in the way things are.
I'm not sure I can or should change.
I feel self-conscious and selfish.

I have to learn somehow
to wait.
Someday I may find my own success—
not dates and clothes
but good feelings about life
helping and giving
real love rather than popularity.

These are hard times though.
Waiting isn't easy.
Help me.

I wish I were good-looking

"You can't judge a book by its cover."
That may be, Lord,
but appearance does make a difference.
The clothes I wear are important.
I feel uncomfortable when I'm not in style.
And people notice good looks.
The good-looking kids get more attention.

But once a cute friend told me
that being good-looking isn't always great either.
When you're cute or beautiful
you sometimes wonder
whether people like *you*
or if they like how you *look*.

I try to keep it straight, Lord.
Kindness and understanding are beautiful.
You have made some people very attractive
but I seldom notice people's looks
when they're listening to me
or caring for me.
People who love other people
are the beautiful ones.

I'm falling in love

I don't think I've ever felt this way before.
I look across a room
and I see his eyes.
He looks straight back at me for a long time—
and my stomach flips!

I think I'm in love.
I want to be near him—
even just talking for a minute between classes
or not talking at all.
And I can tell he feels the same way.

This is a stronger feeling than I've ever had before.
My whole body tingles sometimes
and I suddenly sigh out loud
when I think of him.
I daydream all the time.

Lord, this feels wonderful!
I don't know what happens next,
but I'm thankful
this is happening to me.
I feel alive!

Sex isn't simple

There are moments, Lord,
when my body
and how it feels
surprise me.

I'm at a new door.
I can tell that my emotions
my body pulses
are powerful.
It scares me to have such strong feelings.
I like it
but I have to do some careful thinking.

Sex isn't simple.
Sex needs guidelines.
Babies aren't just cute.
They need responsible parents.
And I am not ready to be a parent yet.

My body is capable of creating a child
and my strong feelings
struggle to overpower
my sense of responsibility.

Help me keep it straight, Lord.
Help me be rational
about future consequences.

I'm glad I can feel this way—
so loving.
Help me take care of myself
and those I love
in a responsible way.

I can't slow down!

I'm always in a hurry—
that's what my folks say.
Don't they understand that
my activities are important to me?
I like being active.
I have lots of energy.

I guess I do get carried away though.
Pretty soon everything seems urgent.
I don't have to do everything this minute.
I don't have to be in every activity
or try every new idea.
But it's hard to choose.
It's hard to say no.
Sometimes it's boring to stay home.

I'm in a hurry.
Where am I going anyway?

They're getting married

They're seventeen
and they're getting married.
She's fussing over her wedding—
gowns
parties
her own sets of towels—
and practicing cooking for him.
He's working overtime
to earn extra money,
to pay for repairs on his car.

I'm happy for them.
She has a pretty ring.
They seem to be so excited.
They've gone together for a long time.
It seems like they know each other well.

A wedding seems a little like a super-prom.
And it would be nice not to worry about
dating
appearances
and all that.

But I wonder if I would want to be married now.
"Married" is for a long time.
What if I changed my mind?
Does it get boring?
How much money does it take?

I guess I'm not ready yet.
I hope they will be happy.
"Married" is for a long time.

Kids are so different

We often sang a song in church school—
"Red and yellow, black and white,
They are precious in his sight.
Jesus loves the little children of the world."
I've been taught that every person
is worthy in God's eyes.
We are equal, but different.

I'll say we're different!
Some kids are shy, some brag,
some like school,
some believe different things from me.
I sometimes have trouble comprehending
that God loves everyone.

I have trouble accepting someone
who is not like me.
It makes me uneasy to be around kids
who are more aggressive
or sophisticated
or who look different from me.
Sometimes I avoid differences,
or judge people on their looks or opinions—
I think I'm better than they are.
I'd like to be able to make everyone
behave and believe like I do.
No waves—no adjustments.

Help me accept their right
to be different from me.
Nobody has all the answers.
We can learn from each other.

I'm old enough!

I'm so tired of being told
I'm not old enough.
All my life—too young!
Too young to go out at night
too young to go on a trip
too young to drive
too young to get a job
too young.
How does anyone expect me to learn
if I'm too young to try?

I'm sorry, Lord.
I'm not patient.
It's really hard to wait.
Help me channel my energy
in ways that show others
I'm responsible.
And help me approach
my parents and others reasonably.
When I beg or shout
I seem immature to them.

It's frustrating to be told
I'm not old enough yet.
"Old enough" seems a long way away.
Help me handle this waiting.

Thanks for the good things

I was feeling sorry for myself
misunderstood
underprivileged
left out.
But you inspired me to try to see my life
from a different point of view.
I began to look for kindness and friendliness.
I thought about
my successes
my health and intelligence
the nice things I have.

I began to see that life is not going to be perfect—
people will not always do what I expect
or fill all my needs.
Things won't always turn out the way I want.

But life and people
often offer me good times,
caring and love.
I'll make a list
and see it in black and white.
My life is full of good things.

It's hard to be poor

I never realized it before.
Things are not equal for people.

I always figured
I would earn enough money
to provide for myself.
All a person has to do is work hard
and she can make it, I thought.
I wondered if poor people were really *trying*.
Weren't they just lazy?

This job has taught me a lot.
I work hard,
but I sure don't earn much money.
I'm lucky I don't need much.

Hal works here, too.
He works hard.
He's worked since he was young
but he never had much.
He has trouble supporting a family
on the wages he earns
even if he works 60 hours a week.

His wife works too—night shifts.
They're tired from working so hard
and always being behind on their bills.
Just when he gets a little ahead
someone gets sick
or his old car needs repair.

His "leisure" time is spent
working overtime
repairing his car
fixing up old equipment.
(My folks just buy new stuff.)
I could never say Hal doesn't try.

Things aren't equal.
Some people start from behind.
I feel lucky.

Why don't I fit in?

I stand apart
looking at the others,
listening to their noise
their music
(my music),
watching their fun,
how they laugh
flirt
kid each other.
I stand alone
and I don't know what to do.

I want to be part of them
but they don't invite me in.
I want to laugh too
but I can't be funny
and I'm afraid to try.

There is a wall of air
between me and them,
an invisible barrier
holding me back.
And the only person
who can
close the distance
try to change
is me—
and I stand apart.

I'm going to run away!

I can't stand it!
I wish I could slam my door
and never have to get along with sisters or brothers
or answer to parents.

Tension.
Arguments.
I can't be myself.
I have to please other people.
It makes me mad!
No one listens to me.
I wish I could leave this place and not come back.

Oh, I'd probably come back . . .
but on my terms.

Who am I kidding?
Leaving means a lot more than
good-bye.
Help me find a way
to cool off
and to get along.
Relationships take a lot of work.

I feel unimportant

Look at all those people
filling the stadium—
kids, old people, families
noisy, drunk, silent, eating.
People!
People all over the world.
And each one
each one
is a person!
who eats dinner
who had a mother
who makes plans
who laughs and cries.

I'll never know them all.
I'll never come near most of them.
I'll never understand
this whole big enormous world.
But they are all there—
individuals.
What will each one do?
What will happen to each of us
separately?
together?

The world is so huge!
How does anyone understand it all
and each part of it
and me?

I feel so small.
Are you there, Lord?

Waiting for my driver's license

If I could only drive!
Won't I ever be old enough?
Waiting for my license takes forever.

I know I can do it—
I could drive today—
but I have to wait.

Why do we always
want things we can't have?
Why does time keep dragging?
And why am I so impatient?

Time is peculiar.
It goes slow when I wait
and fast when I'm having fun.
Help me remember
that time
and life
will pass.
What counts is what I do
right now
this moment.

I will get my license.
The question is
what will I do with my life
between now
and then.

Victory!

I'm so proud!
We won!
I'm smiling
and laughing
even crying a little.
It feels so good to win!

It isn't just good luck—
it takes hard work to be the best.
Cooperation
determination
practice
sacrifice—
they are all big words
and they add up to big victory!

Winning is now.
It's a short-lived high.
What really matters is
what it takes to win.
Winning doesn't mean much
without honesty
without consideration
without gratitude.

Thanks!
Make us respectful
understanding
and kind winners.

What about drinking?

It's supposed to be a big deal
to go on a beer bust.
Some kids love to get drunk.

But kids aren't really funny
when they're drunk.
They act silly
get sick
say stupid things.
What makes me worry
is when they do it
over and over again.

I never knew kids could be alcoholics
but they can.
It isn't just parents who change
from just liking a drink
to the disease of not being able
to say no to alcohol.
Kids can also lose their ability to choose—
they can become dependent on drinking.

I'm glad there are Al-Anon, Alateen,
and Alcoholics Anonymous.
Those groups can help.
Kids can go to them
if they have a drinking problem
or if their folks do.
Drinking is not a joking matter, Lord.

Is it so great to be young?

I sure get tired of adults saying,
"Oh, how nice it must be to be young!"
I don't think being young is so great.
It seems to me that everything is mixed up.
Just when I feel good about school
I mess up a test
or I have to change classes.
I get excited about sports
and then I forget about curfews.
I want to work
but I'm told I'm "too young."
I feel goofy
and I'm told to "act my age."

My friends are really important to me
but we let each other down too.
My parents are great one week
but the next week they crack down.

Being this age is confusing.
I don't know why adults think I'm so carefree.
I'm not.
In fact, I'd rather have more responsibility
like they do.
But I can't decide what I want to do!
I wish I didn't have to think about it.

I hope I get through this stage pretty soon.
Stay with me, okay?

Thanks for different churches

I've always been curious about other churches.
When I was small I visited a friend's church once
but I didn't understand what was happening.

Today was interesting—
a different routine
some new music
another way of praying.
I like to look at worship from a new viewpoint.
It helps me get out of my old rut.

It seems to me
that unless we look carefully
at our pattern
our style
and sometimes compare it
to something else,
we take it for granted.
We tune out even the excellent things.
We get stale.

Thank you, Lord, for differences.

Divorce is hard

My friend is so hostile
so angry and bitter.
His parents got a divorce.

They always fought
or seethed with resentment
and made everyone unhappy.
He told me how scary it was.
I thought he'd feel relieved they broke up
but he's upset.
He isn't happy either way.

I heard once
that kids sometimes feel guilty or responsible
when their parents separate.
Maybe he feels responsible.
Maybe he just feels lost—
insecure
divided by their differences
torn in his loyalties.

Divorce is hard for everyone.
Parents don't like it either.
Kids can get hurt.
I guess he needs my friendship.

Grass—who needs it!

I just had to get out of there.
I could smell that sweet, heavy smell
the minute I got in the door.
I turned around and left.

I don't need it, Lord.
I don't need the manufactured high.
I get my highs
sailing down a ski slope
or playing my guitar alone.
I don't need pot
to feel friendly
or loved—
people do that for me,
not chemicals.

But I was too surprised to say anything.
I just left.
Maybe my leaving said it for me.

I think I made the best choice.
Even when it isn't perfect
I choose reality.

I'm losing a friend

I'm losing a friend
and I feel left out.
Something must be wrong with me.
I used to be good enough,
now I'm not.

We used to do all sorts of things together—
bowl or walk or swim
and especially talk.
We could depend on each other.
Did I do something wrong?
Should I try to act differently?

Things change.
People change.
A friend finds a new friend
or a new activity.
I never see my fifth grade friends anymore.
Nobody did anything "wrong."
We tried new things.
We changed.

Help me not to be discouraged
or frightened
when life and people change.
I change too.
If I let it, maybe losing this friend
will lead me to something better.
Help me to accept change
and to go on.

We lost

It's over.
It's over, and we lost.
All our dreams—
how we would get the trophy
how we would be number one
number one!
The dreams died
in sickening silence.
We lost.

I feel miserable, Lord.
I'm mad at myself for dreaming
because it makes the emptiness more terrible.
I'm sad for the people
who feel responsible for losing.
I'm afraid of tomorrow
with nothing to look forward to.

Help me straighten things out.
This must be
how the disciples felt on Good Friday.
I can't give up—they didn't.
I have to try again
enjoy wishing again—
appreciate all the good times
and victories that come
in games
in relationships
in life.

Help me live with winning or losing.
The defeat is over.
Tomorrow is another day.

Am I superstitious?

Sometimes I twist my apple stem
to see what boy's initial comes up.
Sometimes I wish on a star.
Sometimes I knock on wood or cross my fingers.

There's nothing wrong with all that.
But life is not a matter of chance.
We don't win ball games
with good luck charms.
I don't get good grades
by wearing certain clothes on test days.
We don't achieve success
by wishing.

We work or study.
We pray for guidance
or support
or good sportsmanship.
But we don't pray for favors
or victory.
God isn't a genie in a bottle,
somebody we call on for wishes.
Faith isn't rituals and charms.

Faith is growing in the belief
that God is always present,
always listening and caring,
confident in our abilities,
encouraging our best efforts,
helping us when we're weak.
Faith isn't magic formulas.

I'm protected from the world

When I look ahead
I feel uneasy.
Life is no picnic.
I don't know if I can cope with
sadness
cruelty
pain
getting old.

I've never had to face hard times.
My family protects me
and provides for me.
I don't know much about
crime
hunger
disasters.
I've hardly even known
people different from me,
people with different standards or backgrounds.

But I can't stand still.
I can't pretend
that all's well
or that I'm self-reliant.
I can't avoid other people's problems
or problems of my own.

I can learn.
Division was a problem
until I tried it.
Walking, talking, reading—
I overcame those.
In fact, they weren't really problems at all—
they were challenges.

Maybe I will be able to handle problems
as long as I'm willing to try.
Stick by me, Lord.

I want good grades

I feel great
when I earn good grades.
It isn't superiority—
I don't need to feel better than other people.
It's satisfaction—
from hard work and sacrifice—
and a sense of relief!

The feeling is temporary though.
I just have to start over again—
new projects
more tests
new goals to set.

Help me keep it straight, Lord.
Grades measure achievement.
But learning is ongoing
everyday.
I want to enjoy new ideas
because learning is part of growing and changing,
not just because I want good grades.
I want to be more than a good student.
I want to be a complete person.

I love driving a car

A car is convenient
and fun
and it impresses other kids.
Driving makes me feel free
independent
mature.
And deep down
I feel powerful.

How powerful am I when I drive?
I control
2000 pounds of machinery.
I can travel at great speed.
I can prove to myself
and others
that I have keen, young reflexes.

And I can make a mistake—
forget that kids run in front of cars
take a highway corner too fast
fail to see another car coming
forget to allow for other drivers' mistakes.

I am powerful.
I can kill with my car.
Guide me.

Life isn't fair

Lord, I'm angry!
Popularity, friends, looks
seem more important
than quality and honesty.
Some people get breaks they don't deserve.
"It's not what you know,
it's who you know."
"It takes money
to make money."

Life isn't fair.
Some people are born poor.
They're always hungry
and they never enjoy life.
Some people can't walk or see.
Some people have unkind parents
or no ability to learn.
"The good die young," they say.

I feel indignant
when I get hurt by unfairness.
I feel sad for the others
who are hungry
or handicapped.
I'm angry—
angry with a creation
that has death
and sadness
and unfairness.

How do I live with it, Lord?
I can change some injustice.
Help me work at that.
I can keep trying,
looking for other opportunities
when things don't work out
fairly for me the first time.

And I have to leave the rest to you, Lord.
I won't give up trying to make the world better,
but somehow I have to understand
that life is not fair.
The world will not be perfect.

Jesus didn't conquer the world
like a mighty king.
He endured unfairness.
He gave to people and the world
even if it meant losing life.
Help me be like him.

I need money

It seems like I never have enough money.
There's always something I need—
clothes
stuff for school
hamburgers and malts.
I don't want to be greedy.
I just want what the other kids have.

I know I have a lot—
more than most people in the world,
more than some kids I know.
Still, I seem to want more.

Help me be sensible.
I could manage my money better.
I'm not suffering and
sometimes I'm selfish.
And sometimes
if I stop to think about it
I like spending money
just to have something to do.

When I'm down I feel better
if I can spend money for something—
it's like buying a present for myself.
I suppose it's okay to buy myself presents
but I can't always spend money to feel better.
I have to be more secure than that.

Keep me honest with myself
and realistic
and unselfish.

I'm fickle

I don't understand myself.
I like one boy
then another.
I have a big crush on someone,
then it wears off
and I find someone else to like.
I watch a boy,
I really like him,
and I sit around hoping he'll notice me.
Then after awhile the feeling is gone.

Love is supposed to last.
People who are in love seem to stay in love.
I just keep changing my mind.

Well, maybe that's all right.
Every boy I like
is a little different from the others.
I may settle down to one later on.
As long as I don't hurt boys
by being dishonest or leading them on,
I guess being fickle is natural.

I don't want to move

We're moving.
I feel miserable.

I love my school.
I know all kinds of kids.
I like my neighborhood.
I feel good here.

I'm scared, I guess.
Making new friends may be hard.
What if I don't fit?
What if people are different?
What if I don't make their swim team?
What if I can't cut it?

We're moving—I can't change that.
The rest of my family will have to adjust too.
I know that I can depend on them
to stick with me while we're settling in.

Even though I don't feel like
being a "good sport"
it won't do any good to complain
or to fight the change.
I'll just have to try
to make the best of the new situation.
Maybe some hidden good will come from it.

Help me work it out.
Help me look at life with hope—
to see change as learning and gaining,
not losing and giving up.

Learning is more than school

Who decided that learning
is English
or math
or history?
Isn't learning
car repair
garden success
and getting along with people?

Learning is trying even hard things—
maybe more than once.
It's relating to people
making myself understood
taking care of myself
managing my own affairs well.

Learning is reading directions
and making something of my own.
And it's enjoying beautiful things—
music, nature, leisure.

Learning is every day
with no one to prod me
except myself.
It's wondering
what life is for
and where I fit
in the growing and changing of humanity.

Learning is realizing
what is temporary
and what lasts
forever.

Help me understand tragedy

What is life, anyway?
I didn't really believe
that tragedy could happen to someone I know.
I thought only people in newspaper stories
became paralyzed.

If it happens to a friend
could it happen to me?
Could it be me in the hospital?
Could I die?

I lie awake
wondering if anybody ever really knows
what causes things like that to happen.
I don't believe we are under a spell
where some magician pronounces punishments
or injuries
or death.
But I can't figure out why things happen.

The question is so big
I don't even know where to search for an answer.
I must keep looking—
the Bible
the church
a prayer.
Help me understand, Lord.

Why do they blame teenagers?

I get so sick of hearing teenagers called
irresponsible and immature.
I'm tired of being put into a group
labeled and accused
because of what other teenagers do.

I wish adults would pay attention
to the good things kids do.
We sponsor benefits and special projects
to help others.
Not all kids are bad drivers.
We have new ideas—
we aren't just rebellious.
Adults label us unfairly!

But then I guess I label adults too.
I put them in groups—
write them off as stubborn or old-fashioned.
Some adults are good listeners,
open to new ideas.
Some adults respect most kids.

Help me remember we're all individuals.
It's easy to group people by their age.
But the truth is
each person's personality and behavior are unique.

I learn from my family

Brothers and sisters
aren't like best friends.
They're just there
in the same house
with the same parents.
I know their quirks.
We've yelled at each other
and fought for the bathroom.
I've felt jealous
or resentful
or proud.
I've wanted to be alone
but I've missed them when I was away.

We learn how to cooperate
by living in families.
It's training ground for life.
We learn to live with each other—
eat and play
go to church
talk or argue—
live.

Lord, help me appreciate
the importance of a family.
In good or bad times,
my family knows me best.
They stand by me
forgive me
and need me to love them too.
Help me love my family.

I feel guilty

When I feel guilty
I'm not myself.
I'm afraid.
I wonder if people like me,
probably because I don't like myself.
I keep thinking about my guilt.
I can't seem to let go—
to get out from under my heavy spirit.
I'm self-centered and miserable.

Other people feel guilty.
Some of them feel guilty most of the time.
I feel sorry for people
who always feel like failures.
They want to be perfect
and can't be.

I know from stories of Jesus
that the answer is asking for forgiveness.
I can ask people to forgive me.
I can forgive myself.

And I can ask God.
He sets me free
because he knows I need help
and he loves me whatever I do.
Whatever I do!
That's a miracle.
It makes me want to do better,
and now I'm not afraid to fail.

Who will listen to me?

There are things I can't talk about.
Odd thoughts—
some of them dumb
some of them disgusting
some of them just random, unexpected.
And questions.
Who can I ask?

Sometimes I can't talk about things I've done.
My parents wouldn't understand
or they'd worry
or they'd think I was crazy.
And I'm not sure if I can tell
some of my friends either.
They might laugh at my ideas.
I'm not always proud of what I think or do.

So what do I do, Lord?
I suppose I can keep some thoughts to myself—
nobody tells everyone everything.
I can discuss some things with friends.
It seems like when I dare
to trust people,
to talk to them,
it turns out
they feel and think and act
like I do.
I'm not unique
or crazy
or weird.

And I can tell you the rest,
the things I don't dare tell anyone else.
Jesus knows
that people have all sorts
of experiences and thoughts.
I can tell you, Lord.
You'll understand.

Fear is part of life

It seems like we expect ourselves
to act confident
and in control
all the time.

I catch myself pretending I'm not afraid
of danger
or loneliness
or failure
or people.
But I'm kidding myself
and deep inside I know it.

In a way
it's part of why I go to church.
I need someplace
someone
who can support me when I'm scared,
who doesn't let me down
or expect superhuman behavior.
In church I can be more honest with myself.

Jesus was reluctant at Gethsemane.
Peter and the other disciples were afraid.
That comforts me.
Fear is part of life.
I don't have to let it take over
so I shut myself off from life.
But I can't pretend
I'm never afraid either.

I hate myself

I bet no one feels like I do.
I feel like a loser.
I make mistakes.
I act dumb.
I yell at my folks.
I disappoint my friends.

Everyone else looks relaxed.
I feel uncomfortable.
Sometimes I talk too much.
Sometimes I can't think of anything to say.
I worry about my clothes.
I can't decide what to do after I graduate.
I get all confused about dating.

Some days
when I feel like this
I wonder what life is for.
Where do I fit?
Help me through this awful self-hate time, Lord.
You promise that you love everyone
even *me*.

He died

Death seemed so far away.
I thought about it
but not too hard.
It was like
dying is for old people—
strangers, mostly,
or grandparents.

I never liked talking about it
and I never wanted to think
about my parents or anyone close to me dying.
Everyone else avoids it too,
using words like
"passed away"
"heavenly home"
"gone for awhile"
"left this earth."
Hardly anyone says "dead."

Kids aren't supposed to die.
We knew he was really sick.
But in high school dying is far away.
Now I have to look at death straight on.

He died.
I say it over and over to myself.
He died.
He's gone.
It happened.
I just don't know what to do.
Sometimes I'm more stunned than sad.
Things are all mixed up.

And suddenly I know
I will die.
It's real.
It happens to people I love.
I need something,
someone bigger than me
to help me cope with this.
What did Jesus say?

What do I do about anger?

I've discovered that anger
has several causes—
frustration
disappointment
feeling unimportant
feeling left out
feeling misunderstood.
It all comes out in anger.

Some people need to pound
slam doors
hit pillows.
Some people spread the anger to others
yelling
seething
paying back
hitting.
Some people pretend—
they don't show their anger
because they think it's wrong.

My anger scares me sometimes.
I want to hit,
hit hard.
An electric shock shoots through me.

Anger is part of life.
We can spread it around
and make everyone unhappy.
We can relish it
enjoy it
keep it alive.

We can pretend we don't feel angry
and push it down inside us
where it will eat away
at our stomach
our personality
our behavior.

Or we can use it
to express ourselves
without blaming
without hurting.
Jesus was angry.
He was even physical about it.
He overturned huge tables.

My anger is part of me.
Help me use it constructively.

Parents aren't perfect

I guess I used to think Mom was perfect.
She gave me advice.
She could do so many things I couldn't do.
She taught me
how to sew
how to swim—
all sorts of things.

It seems like she's different now.
I notice all her mistakes.
Sometimes she embarrasses me
and sometimes I don't like her.
She isn't perfect at all.

What's happening?
Has Mom changed?
Or am I changing?
I hate myself
when I criticize her behind her back,
and I think I hurt her feelings
when I criticize her to her face.
I forget she can be hurt too.

But it scares me to find out
the person I depended on all these years
isn't perfect.
Nobody's perfect.

Then I begin to wonder
who *can* I depend on?
Who won't let me down?
Stay with me, Lord.
I know I can depend on you.

Is it all right to doubt?

I never had these thoughts before—
wondering if there *is* God,
doubting the divinity of Christ.
I always took all that teaching for granted.
"It must be true
because my teachers
and parents
and pastors
said so."

I sort of like thinking about all this
but it scares me.
Am I an unbeliever—
an atheist?
Am I an agnostic—
a doubter
bound up in questioning?
Is it all right to wonder?

The disciples were not always sure.
The disciples questioned too.
Jesus didn't reject them.
He understood.

If this is part of faith—
testing it for myself—
stay with me, Lord.
I can't run away from doubts.
Help me deal with them.

I don't understand cruelty

Cruelty isn't just
murder
torture
violence.
Cruelty is
harsh words
meanness
rejection.
I don't understand cruelty.

One of the girls at school is different.
She acts dumb sometimes.
I don't understand her very well.
The kids are cruel.
Boys laugh at her and tease her
and girls snicker behind her back.
She's almost always alone.

I feel sorry for her.
Feeling alone is awful.
No one likes being teased.
She acts even stranger
when she feels rejected.
I've tried to be friendly.
It's hard.
Other kids probably wonder
why would I like *her?*

I have to try though.
I can't stand their cruelty.
It's wrong.
People need kindness and caring.
I know I can't make up for her personality
and I can't fill her whole need for friends.
But I can be sensitive.
I can try to understand.
Everyone needs kindness.

I'm bored

I'm tired of school—
the same routine
the same friends.
Tired of my family.
Tired of myself.
Tired of life.
I feel uninspired.
Nothing is new or exciting.

It scares me to be so uninvolved and uninterested.
I wonder if I'll spend my whole life
feeling dull, distant.

Lord,
am I letting a temporary lull become
overwhelming?
Is there a way I can get back in touch
with life
with personalities
with fresh ideas
with all kinds of feelings?

Help me open up my eyes
so I see more of life
and make good use of it
rather than wasting it
on boredom.

I'm so immature

I blew it!
I just cannot act sophisticated
like the others.
They seem so grown up.
I do dumb things.

My parents keep reminding me to
grow up
be mature
act more sensibly
be responsible.

I intend to do all those things
and then I do something really stupid.
I don't even mean to
but I do.
The other kids think I'm immature—
and so do I!

Help me figure myself out, Lord.
I guess I don't understand
everything about myself.
I guess I am growing up gradually.

I need patience
and I need help
so I learn from my mistakes.

I feel alone

Loneliness scares me.
It's so empty.
It surrounds me
and intimidates me.
I can feel lonely at a school dance
or at the dinner table.
Sometimes I feel lonely
with my best friend!

It seems to me
that I didn't feel so alone when I was younger.
I felt close to Mom and Dad.
I had a lot of fun with friends.
Now I feel less secure.
I feel alone.

Help me understand this part of life, Lord.
Help me reach out beyond myself
to you
to others
so I begin to find ways
to satisfy the hunger
of loneliness.

Adults are so sure

It looks to me like adults have it made.
They believe.
They say it correctly.
They know about all those Bible stories.
They tell about how faith helped them.

They're so sure—
and that makes me uncomfortable.
I'm not that sure.
I have doubts.
I do all kinds of things
I'm not proud of.

I wonder if they ever feel like me.
Or do they always feel faithful?
Maybe I ought to ask one of them.

Do people like me?

I keep wondering, "Do people like me?"
Will they accept me
no matter what I wear
or what I look like?
Am I pleasant to be around?
Am I smart enough?
Do people like my sense of humor?

I get very tired sometimes,
trying to please people.
I'm not always on my best behavior—
kind, polite, cheerful.
Will people reject me
if I relax or act dumb sometimes?
Do people like me just as I am?

Lord, there are some things about me
that I don't like.
Help me change
my bad habits
and my selfishness.
But help me
be who I am and enjoy myself too.
I'm the only "me" there is
and I am of value to the world.

I don't have to please people.
I only have to accept my limitations
and enjoy my gifts and opportunities.
People like me when I'm natural
and when I show them I like them too.

I dread getting old

Lord,
I can't avoid getting old,
but I dread it.
I don't want to feel left out
or babied
or frustrated by illness.

Some old people are great!
My grandpa was so much fun
and my grandmother listens so well.
She's patient with me.

But some old people seem unhappy.
They look lonely or they can't move around much.
They're sick or dying.

It seems to me that we ignore old people.
We're so busy and fast-moving.
They need friendship.
I could make an effort
to be friendly with old people.
I could even visit a lonely old person
instead of worrying about my old age.
I'd enjoy being with someone older
for a change.

I can act out my concern today
instead of dreading the future.

Happy Easter!

Easter—
sunshine, fresh air,
dew glistening on the grass
Easter—
not eggs and candy
but a colorful celebration
of the chance Jesus gave me
to start over again.
Easter means he will
forgive any mistakes
and give me new life—
every day.

Easter is happy
because Easter is always new,
always fresh.
I never have to give up
because Jesus never stopped living
and never stops loving me.
Happy Easter!

I need time alone

This is a good time—
sitting alone
looking at the trees,
no responsibilities
no pressure
quiet.

The world is beautiful.
Time doesn't matter.
No one to impress
no rules
no problems.
Peace.

I needed this break.
Thanks, Lord.

Help me accept compliments

I was really surprised.
I couldn't say anything at first.
A compliment catches me off guard.

Sometimes I want a compliment very much.
I need praise.
I spend time and money on clothes
hoping for admiration.

But other times I'm embarrassed.
I end up apologizing
or denying the compliment—
"It was nothing," or
"You don't have to say that."

I don't know why I say things like that.
It's nice to realize that someone admires
or respects
or appreciates me.
It feels good.
It makes me want to do well again.
I guess it's rude not to say thank you
when someone goes to the trouble
of praising me.

Help me accept praise.
A compliment helps me
learn more about myself
and about those who offer it to me.

What's my future?

Lord,
what in the world am I going to do?
I feel pressured.
Time is moving.
Everyone keeps asking me about my plans.
It seems like I'm supposed to know
but I don't.
All I have in my head are questions.
Will I go to college?
What will be my job?
Do I ever want to get married?
If I let myself imagine
twenty, forty years ahead
I'm overwhelmed.

Mom and Dad have their ideas
of what is best for me.
But I'm me—
I have to decide.
Help me be unafraid to risk a decision.
A decision isn't forever,
but it's a start.
Don't let me decide
out of rebellion
or without thinking for myself.

Help me think things through
thoroughly
looking at all possibilities.
Help me sort things out.
I know you'll be there
wherever I go.

Christmas seems different now

I miss being a child at Christmastime.
It was fun believing in Santa Claus
getting presents
having school vacation.
Now I feel let down.
Even though I enjoy
having my own money to buy gifts
and going to special parties,
the thrill and excitement are gone.

Lord, help me find new meaning in Christmas.
Maybe I'm looking for the wrong things.
I can find pleasure and excitement
in doing something for someone else
making little children happy
spending time talking with friends.
I can give as well as receive.
I can start to think
about the deep meanings of this season.

Christmas can be more than a child's excitement.
The real Christmas is about the Child.

I hurt my parents

I feel guilty.
I hurt my parents—
not just today
but many times.
I'm selfish or stubborn,
late or moody.
I say whatever I feel
and I hurt them.

I'm sorry, Lord.
I want to be independent
and sometimes that gets the best of my judgment.
I know I could be more patient and kind.

Help me do the hardest thing of all.
Lord, help me tell them
I'm sorry.

I'm not perfect

When I was small
failure meant ugly red checks
beside wrong answers.

Failure seems much worse now.
Then I could correct the answers
and see that I had learned.
Now I can't always
make up for mistakes.
Now failure is more a feeling
than a red mark.

Help me, Lord,
to live with imperfection.
I'm not perfect
and some things I can't do well.

But a mistake isn't forever either.
Jesus put his life on that.

Help me try again—
like that serenity prayer:
"God grant me the serenity
to accept the things I cannot change,
courage to change the things I can,
and wisdom to know the difference."

Sometimes I daydream

I'm getting an award for good grades.
I'm the boss of my own company.
I'm the best skier or a famous singer.
I'm rewarded for my service
at the hospital or in government.
I save someone's life.

Daydreaming is a nice pastime.
It makes me feel important and worthwhile.
I get away from problems.

But I can't live on dreams.
They always come to an end.
Reality reappears
and I'm back to being myself—
jobs to do
books to study
rooms to clean
practice to go to.

Dreams don't come true
without hard work.
I'd better get busy.
Right, Lord?

Dishonesty is more than stealing

There are different kinds of dishonesty.
Cheating on a test and shoplifting are dishonest.
But pretending I like people I don't even respect
is dishonest too.

Sometimes, just to feel liked,
I act in ways that are cruel
or just out of character for me.
I act like I'm not smart
because it's not cool to be smart.
I pretend one of the boys is funny
when I think he's just showing off.
That's dishonest too.

Sometimes I kid myself—
tell myself that I'm not angry
when I'm furious inside.
I pretend that I'm not hurt
if a boy stops paying attention to me,
when I feel sad and disappointed.

Lord, help me be honest.
I don't want to pretend I like things
that offend or bore me,
things that aren't right.
I can politely disagree.
Most of all, Lord,
help me develop the courage
to be honest with myself—
to accept my feelings or failings,
and to be true to my personality
my values
my faith.

I'm disgusted with myself

I made such a dumb mistake!
I forgot I'd promised to be there.
If I can't remember important things
how can I expect myself to
become a parent
or hold down a job?
I'm disgusted with myself.

But Mom didn't even get mad!
I guess she figured
I had scolded myself enough
so she didn't need to.
She just said,
"Nobody's perfect.
You'll have to meet another time."

I feel better.
She expects me to be capable
(so I'll try)
but she knows I make mistakes too.
I was too hard on myself.
The whole point of the good news
is that no one is perfect
but God accepts us anyway.
It's a great message.
It makes me want to do my best
without fear of rejection
if I fail.

What can one person do?

The world belongs to millions of people.
Many are sick and hungry.
Most of them live with large families
on poor land
in unhealthy conditions.
How can I change that?
I'm only one person.

The earth is no longer clean and fresh.
But what can one person do?

People are hurt
by unfair treatment
war
mental illness.
People need help and kindness.
But I am one person,
only *one*.
I feel small
unimportant
ineffective
against all those problems.

Still, when I think about it,
I know that I'm careless.
My candy wrapper adds to the clutter.
I have bad habits—
eating too much
not sharing
driving when I could walk
not learning about voting.
Why should anyone else care
if I don't?

I can't houseclean the whole world, Lord.
But I can do something about my corner,
care about the ground and the air.
I can show that I care about people—
that I want to end their suffering.

Jesus cared for everyone.
I'm only me, Lord,
but I want to be
the best me I can
with your help.

Everything is tomorrow

Study now so you can get a job tomorrow.
Tomorrow you'll need to know this.
Tomorrow you'll want loyal friends.
Tomorrow you'll be glad for good saving habits.

I'm tired of tomorrow.
I am today.
Tomorrow never comes—
there's always another tomorrow to wait for.
I'm sick of thinking about my future
and planning and predicting.
I live now.
I want to enjoy now.
I want to feel now—
sadness
happiness
kindness—
now.

Why do I go to church?

I feel numb to all of this—
singing, praying, sermon.
I'm not involved.
I don't really want to be here.

Where do I want to be, Lord?
In the future?
That never comes.
It always turns into today.
In the past?
It was fun being a kid
but I'd rather make my own decisions.

So here I am in the present.
I can't concentrate—
but I'm not trying.
Maybe I can read the hymnal
or tune in on the sermon.
Maybe there's something there for me.
I won't know
if I don't snap into it
and try.

Every worship experience
doesn't have to be like a TV spectacular.
Maybe a church service is significant
because it allows me time
to muse
to think
to be with people I enjoy
to feel like I'm part of something greater,
a believing group.

What is grown up?

What is it, to grow up?
To get strong enough or old enough to work?
To understand that work is always part of life
and that doing something well
makes me feel good?
To have the answers to things like faith?
Or to know that questions
will keep appearing?

Does "grown up" mean drudgery
and responsibility?
Or can responsibility sometimes be fun
and feel satisfying?

Is "grown up"
twenty-one
eighteen
or every year in different ways?
My parents are grown up—
but their problems don't end
and they don't have
all the answers.

Is grown up secure?
Or do we always doubt ourselves
and feel uneasy in new situations?

Maybe growing up means
not to expect
perfect
smooth
carefree lives—
not to give up
or run away
when things get rough.

I've never thought this way before.
I've never tried to look deeply at life—
not until now.
Maybe I'm growing up!

What does confirmation mean?

Confirm.
Dad confirms reservations at a hotel
by saying, "Yes, I'm coming."
Mom confirms an RSVP
by calling a hostess
to say, "Yes, we will attend."
A computer confirms my estimate
by typing, "Keep trying.
You're on the right track."

Now I'm ready to confirm my intentions—
not to a hotel or hostess or computer
but to God.

Sometimes I can't take it seriously.
I feel self-conscious
even silly.
My mind wanders
when our pastor is explaining or giving directions.
And sometimes I wonder
if I should be going through with this.
I mean, do I know enough?
Do I believe enough?
Do I really have faith?

But pastor said
we are always growing as Christians
we have ups and downs
we never know it all
we are always learning
but
we are always accepted
always loved.

If faith is believing God always loves me,
then I'm on the right track, Lord.
I intend to keep trying
to attend
to grow.

This is to confirm
that I accept your invitation, Lord.

What is the Way?

I'm not always happy.
Is it all right to be sad?
Is sadness something I should avoid?
Does feeling sad
mean something is wrong with me?

God promises peace—
but what is peace?
Should life be smooth?
If turmoil comes
should I run away?

Sometimes I experience the fruits
of kindness, joy, peace, love.
Peace usually comes with kindness and love.
But once, after I yelled at the kids who were cruel
I felt all peaceful inside.

How can I be sure what is loving—
to speak
to be silent
to take a serious step
to hold back and wait?
What if I never know?
What if I make a mistake?
How will I feel peaceful then?

I can test what I do
by what Jesus did.
Jesus did not act helpless.
He took steps to change things
loved openly
cried
got angry.
He listened
confronted
trusted
knew the Father.
And he forgave everyone—
even me!

What a powerful example for me.
Thank you, Lord,
for understanding
and for showing me the Way.